Ben Kavanagh

Ben Kavanagh was born in 1989, in Hampshire, UK. He attended Collingwood College School before training at the University of Cambridge, graduating in 2011 with an MA Hons in English, Drama & Education.

Since then Ben has worked as an actor, director, writer, podcaster and educator, both in the UK and internationally.

He is also the founder and current Artistic Director of Clatterhouse Theatre, a company which produces theatre which is rich, arresting and above all makes noise. Combining powerful performances and ensemble work with quirky high concept and design, the company likes to make noise by championing new writing and reinventing the classics, both for the purposes of challenging contemporary audiences whilst also giving them a memorable and fulfilling experience.

The Convert is Ben's first published play.

First published in the UK in 2022 by Aurora Metro Publications Ltd.

67 Grove Avenue, Twickenham, TW1 4HX

www.aurorametro.com   info@aurorametro.com

FB/AuroraMetroBooks Twitter @aurorametro
Instagram aurora_metro

With many thanks to: Saranki Sriranganathan

Printed in the UK by 4edge printers on sustainably resourced paper.

ISBNs:

(print) 978-1-912430-76-5

(ebook) 978-1-912430-77-2

by

Ben Kavanagh

AURORA METRO BOOKS

Dedicated to Evan and Paige

CONTENTS

About the Company 6

Cast and Creative Team 7

Playwright's Note 8

THE CONVERT 17

Above The Stag Theatre is an independent Charity and Theatre Company serving the LGBT+ community and its supporters.

We believe that telling and hearing stories is a fundamental human need and that the LGBT+ community deserves a voice. We provide a platform for this voice through the production of plays, musicals, cabaret, readings, comedy and entertainment in all its forms. We strive for excellence across all these disciplines.

We look to the future by developing new work and new audiences within our community and friends as well as producing or hosting revivals and classics.

Equality is at the heart of our mission and the spaces we inhabit will always be safe spaces for everyone. We seek to create an environment where LGBT+ people and our supporters can mix across any perceived boundaries of age, gender, disability, race or any other arbitrary means of discrimination.

www.abovethestag.org.uk

THE CONVERT

by Ben Kavanagh

The Convert was first presented at the Above the Stag Theatre, London, on Wednesday 8th June, 2022 with the following company:

Cast

Ben Kavanagh – Arbiter
Nick Mower – Alix
Sam Goodchild – Marcus

Production Team

Ben Kavanagh – Writer
Gene David Kirk – Director
Andy Hill – Producer
John Owen – Executive Producer
David Shields – Design
James Whitmarsh – Production Manager
George Reeve – Video Design
Joseph Ed Thomas – Lighting Design
Paul Gavin – Sound Design
Joel Kendall – Stage Manager/Operator
Ian Massa-Harris – Make-up
Derek Benfield – Production Assistant
Jon Bradfield – Poster / Programme Design
PBG Studios – Production Photography

PLAYWRIGHT'S NOTE
Ben Kavanagh

The Convert, whilst being an engaging piece of theatre live, presents several problems on the page which are almost always best overcome by individual companies in the rehearsal room and the theatre. Having had the benefit of working on the play twice in its earliest inceptions has afforded me some perspective of what might be called, 'fundamental constants', which, if followed, allow for the play to find its full potential. I include them below for companies to take note of, so that they may safeguard the artistic integrity of the piece and realise real success with it. Something which shouldn't be underestimated when tackling a play with such a serious subject matter.

Conversion Therapy

There are too many types of conversion therapy to include in one evening at the theatre. I tried many types in different versions and found that some lent themselves to theatricality more than others and I feel comfortable writing that, that was my primary concern from the outset. Presenting torture is delicate – you want your audience to be horrified but ultimately to take it in and its accompanying messages. Be in no doubt though, 90% of the torture and therapies in the play are based on real conversion techniques. Where they are not, they have been stretched and constructed from the general animosity and marginalising that LGBTQ+ people face every day, and when this does occur, it is always for dramatic purpose.

For instance, I know of no conversion technique that involves blinding. However, I know that in some cultures, lesbians have been found to have been raped as a way to correct their sexuality, with the rapists blinding them after, so that the victim cannot identify the perpetrator, should they be brave enough to go to the authorities. Whilst blinding has no direct link to the correction in this instance, and is more of a post act, it clearly has a link with the torture and oppression of LGBTQ+ people and so justifies it's place amongst other, more direct techniques. Blinding Alix in the play serves to highlight this, but is also symbolic of Alix's inability to see the facility and Marcus for what they are, as well as being a literal physicalising of the facility trying to stop the love between the pair.

The World

The setting of the play gives a lot of people (including myself on occasions) a headache. The action clearly involves technological advances that would be impossible to produce today, so the temptation would be to set the play in the future. Whilst this makes immediate logical sense, it is less evocative dramatically. Setting the play in the future allows a distance between the audience and the subject matter that takes away its power. Conversion therapy continues today, so to present it alongside future technologies in an overly colourful "future world" might lead to the misinterpretation that it is not as severe or present in contemporary society. It is.

My suggestion therefore is to set it as far as possible, in all aspects, in the present day but imagine that it is a parallel universe where technological advances have been made quicker. Make the characters and the world reachable by the audience, even though it has many unfamiliar qualities, and you will preserve the political dynamic and social commentary inherent in every fibre of the play.

Music, Sound and Scene Changes

The play is very specific in terms of music choices for good reason and these should be adhered to entirely. This world is not a colourful one and the inputting of music, however stirring or lyrically "relevant", should be avoided at all times. Sound is different though. One of the great strengths and weaknesses of the play is its "Seesaw" format. As a strength, the constant flipping between the RED and the BLUE room give it a relentless feeling, and puts us into Alix's mind-numbingly narrow life. The rooms are isolating and whilst we always know where we are going next, the potential of what the room holds for us is increasingly dramatic.

For the RED room the transaction of violence increases through the play and in the BLUE room the transaction of love increases. This is all worthy. The weakness though is in the lack of the broader world, most notably the wider facility. Design therefore, must play a pivotal role in creating that facility. I would suggest mostly through sound, light and scene change.

In the original draft, I wrote a detailed description of the sound in every scene change stage direction but after the play's first production almost none of it matched completely and I have since felt that this sort of thing is likely to change dramatically from production to production and so I should be less prescriptive in the actuality and realising of it.

All I would say, is that we must get a sense of the size of the facility, of its living quality, of its perpetual danger, and of it as a means of consistent surveillance. Much like the house in Stephen King's *The Shining*, it's best to think of the facility as the fourth character of the play, which is only able to speak and make itself known, during the scene changes. Computers tapping, people walking, shadows passing by doors, are all the sort of dramatic fodder that will make it work. If music is to be used, it should be almost filmic in quality: no words, atmospheric and emotive, echoing and commenting always on the scene it's come from or the scene it is going to.

Characters

In relation to the characters of the play, there isn't a huge amount to suggest beyond what is already conveyed in the script itself and certainly the script should be the first port of call for interpretation. Regardless, I've put some thoughts down which might be beneficial to the actors of the company.

Alix is very much the centre of the play. He should be the youngest of the three, energised and misbelieving of the way society views his "condition". There is a temptation to play him as plucky because of his occasionally dry tone and sarcastic outlook, but though he has no concept of what the facility is like at the outset, he is, deep down, scared and nervous about what exactly his treatment will entail. His journey moves from being somewhat content to be removed from a society that rejects him (some of whom are his closest family), to longing to be back with them, if just for a moment. Sometimes this journey is the relentless, perhaps inevitable, struggle between these two ideas – that of who he used to be and that of who he wishes to be. The chief focus of the character though, is the progression and development of the violence enacted on him and his subsequent pain management and his realisation of what love means to him. I have outlined more thoughts on both in sections below.

Marcus is an interesting character in that the audience come to know (and so does the actor on the first read) that he is a simulation. He's not real, in any real sense, at all. The actor could go back and forth, time and again, trying to decide how to play this. My advice would be to give whatever backstory you need to get to a real performance, but in no way hint to the audience that he isn't what he seems. The most important part of the play is that the audience believe that Alix and Marcus' love is real.

Indeed, at the end, it matters not to Alix that Marcus is a real person – the most important thing is that through loving him, Alix has come to accept that the love is natural, viscerally real, and the only thing worth living for.

In terms of dynamic, Marcus should be older and physically more dominating than Alix. This creates a dramatic frisson; Alix is younger and more delicate than Marcus but fights his incarceration, whilst Marcus is older, broader and more powerful but seems completely socialised into the facility. In this dynamic, both have something to teach each other and therefore the growing of their relationship makes more sense and, hopefully, paves the way for love in the audience's mind.

The Arbiter is a faceless amalgamation of several archetypes. He's designed specifically to represent all the different types of oppressive people, which marginalised people come to experience in their struggle: unaccepting parents, dogmatic religious leaders, legislating monarchs and politicians, conversion founders and torturers, and more, can all be found in the various lines uttered by the Arbiter, and sometimes presented in whole scenes.

Ultimately, the most interesting moment is when Alix suggests the Arbiter himself is gay. This is not an uncommon phenomenon, that in the deepest hearts of prejudice, lies the desire for a secret truth very close to the prejudice itself. In the play, it's easily explained away. Alix comes to find that the entire play is a series of tests, from the moment he arrives into the facility and so, naturally, it could be assumed the Arbiter's kiss may well be just another test. Or it may not. I'll leave that for the actor playing the part, and the director leading the company, to decide, as it doesn't have any dramatic effect on what the audience sees, only what the actor feels. In this instance, whatever they may need to get them to the intention of the moment is justifiable and has not only my blessing, but my whole-hearted support.

Set Pieces

There are difficult and alienating set pieces in the play which require careful consideration, and often intricate choreography and design, to stage successfully. I would ask companies to start from the outset by making a clear distinction between 'actual reality' and 'theatrical reality' and place the set pieces into either camp before staging.

The Convert is undoubtedly a piece of New Brutalism or In-Yer-Face theatre and yet, if all of the blood in the play were to be realised only symbolically (like in Sarah Kane's *Cleansed*, where lopped-off hands are most often presented with actors holding long red ribbons) it would lose much of its impact. In this instance then, a sense of 'actual reality' should be the company's main objective.

However, when Alix and Marcus are making love or when Alix is blinded – 'theatrical reality' would be more appropriate because of the extremis of the action. For instance, if a realistic presentation of the blinding is chosen – the Arbiter delving into Alix's eye and pulling out the ball King Lear style, you're likely to find audiences will look away, and thus the impact is lost; and in terms of the love scene, well, audiences find sex funny. There's no other way of putting it. If companies choose the reality of the situation (and this is something we found when presenting the play, the first time) you're likely to get a lot of awkward and embarrassed giggles, taking the audience outside of some of the most important action of the play:

Alix and Marcus physically realising their love fully. These are just two examples but there are many to tackle in the script and they mustn't be overlooked or underestimated. The distinction between what would actually happen and what is the best reality when presented in a theatre, in front of an audience, is an extremely important one, and difficult conversations should be welcomed in the pursuit of presenting the play in the best possible way.

The Development of Pain

Of all the set pieces in the play, the hardest is chronicling the effect of the violence on Alix, not in terms of make-up, but in terms of the performance of pain. Companies must work hard to decrease Alix's threshold throughout the piece until at the end he is a shell of his former self, completely broken. He is a martyr for his cause and if he is seemingly as sarcastic, dry and plucky at the end as at the beginning but just with a sling on, then the play loses all it's impact. By the end he should be a shaking mess, swollen, covered in blood and bruises, blinded by the dimmest of light, and blown over by the smallest breeze.

Love

The first short work-in-progress production of *The Convert*, staged as part of the CONTACT season at Above The Stag Theatre in 2021, involved a post-show symposium. It was an enlivening experience to hear audiences talk about my play, but I was taken aback by one question about whether or not the season would involve any plays which were more "hopeful and positive about LGBT+ experiences". I felt I had to chime in to say that, at its centre, this play, like all good theatre is a love story which *is* hopeful.

Its themes and subject matter provide a stark warning of the dangers of by-standing when such atrocities are committed under our nose. Therefore, hopefully audiences will feel emboldened to seek out injustice and crimes against humanity, and to do something about them.

The torture of Alix and the depiction of conversion techniques, whilst they are real and visceral, should only ever be treated as the underscore to the relationship between Alix and Marcus. It is simply not sustainable, to hold an audience for two hours on torture and violence alone. If that was all *The Convert* was, then it would be little more than a piece of voyeurism, fetishizing conversion therapy, fit for little more than a Netflix documentary. The power of the torture arises from being placed in direct opposition to the emerging love of the protagonist and his cell mate.

Alix is sent to the facility to learn that the way he was born to love is wrong and invisible, therefore the greatest gift Marcus gives him with his love, whether he is real or not, is the realisation that his love is worthy, that it matters. And that in turn is why Alix's death, whilst certainly upsetting, is hopeful. Alix does not fight when he goes to the Other Place. Why? He is happy to go because he knows that there is nothing to return to, should he be allowed to go back to the society.

All he has, is who he is, which like all of us, is defined almost entirely by the way we love each other. When he accepts himself, he is happy to die. He is therefore a martyr, and whilst they often have different motives, martyrs always represent hope, because their deaths mark causes that will be seen and felt for generations. Alix can die happy because he can hold his head up and die accepting himself.

Companies ignore this at their peril.

THE CONVERT

Ben Kavanagh

Characters:

ARBITER
ALIX
MARCUS

Setting:

The action takes place in a technologically advanced facility. Present day, but in a parallel universe.

Notes On Formatting & Parts

A / at the end of a line, indicates a hard cue bite for the following line.

The distinction between stage directions related to held moments between dialogue is a difficult one to decide and can take up valuable time for companies. For the benefit of speed, companies may like to use the below guide to improve the rehearsal process. They are included here in time order (the fastest first) and with descriptions.

... An ellipsis denotes a character's hesitation.

Beat. A literal beat for breath.

Pause. The characters have nothing to say for a short time.

Long Pause. The characters have nothing to say for an extended period of time.

Silence. Timewise, the same as a long pause, but instead of there being an absence of dialogue, silence sits in place of dialogue. Much is being said in silence, though nothing out loud.

The play is split into two parts rather than two acts because it runs continuously from scene to scene with no real need for stopping. I therefore include the sign posting of the parts, so that the play may be played in one sitting or in two parts with an interval, whichever suits the company and theatre presenting the play best.

PART ONE

1

Darkness. And then a video, projected on the back wall.

ARBITER Hmmm. That's an interesting question. I suppose it depends what you mean by desired outcomes. People come to us because they want to change their lives, and not just because the law now requires it. Because they want a better chance. You see, in the past, there was a concerted effort to understand difference within an unrealistic framework. That is to say that one should define and understand somebody's ability to function in a lawful and healthy manner, by measuring the extent to which society accepts that difference. As if, everybody simply understanding each other without any real reference points was at all possible. But even if it was, what use is that? Correction and its ultimate desired effect which is complete conversion, gives the patient a second chance. Now, if you wish to use their level of difference at the end of the programme as a measurement of desired outcome then yes, sure, the methods don't work... because the patient's difference isn't changed, but what if you measure their life chances? What if you measure their quality of life? Well, that changes exponentially. Our patients come to us different, and they either return to this place as one of us all – healthy, happy, hopeful, straightened out – if you'll pardon the pun, or they are removed to the Other Place where the rest of them who cannot... who cannot... find their way, go. I like to think about difference as a condition. I think illness is a crass simile but condition seems to suit. The condition is delusion. The delusion that this is natural. That they don't have a choice. Luckily for us, their own delusion can be used against them, using effective medicine. I am the medicine.

Blackout.

2

Lights up on the Red Room. ALIX sits alone in half-light. He thinks. The ARBITER enters.

ARBITER   Stand up please.

ALIX stands.

ARBITER   Thank you for compliance. I can see you're going to do very well.

ALIX   Thank you.

ARBITER   Don't reply unless I ask, okay?

ALIX says nothing. He stares at the ARBITER, who looks on expectantly. Eventually...

ALIX   Yes/

ARBITER   No. You replied again. Dear me, I thought you were going to be an easy one. Let's have a system, shall we? Tell me, do you remember when you used to go to primary school and you needed the toilet, you'd put your hand up, wouldn't you? Say, "yes".

ALIX   "Yes."

ARBITER   Well here, we don't put hands up. If I require an answer, I'll give you permission to give it. If you want to speak or ask a question, then you can open your mouth like so. (*The Arbiter opens his mouth wide, his eyes wild and bulging. He returns* *to a friendly smile.)* Say you are "happy" and this is "agreeable to you".

ALIX "I'm happy and this is agreeable to me."

ARBITER That's much better. We're getting along now, aren't we. Say, "yes".

ALIX "Yes."

ARBITER Say, "we're going to be the best of friends."

ALIX "We're going to be the best of friends."

ARBITER Steady on, Alix, we've only just met. You can't go around making friends with any Dick, Harry or Tom. You'll appear fickle. You're not a fickle person are you Alix? Say, "No".

ALIX "No."

ARBITER Glad to hear it. Because I've read your notes. You say what you mean. You give everything to what you do. You don't go around making idle promises that might hurt people's feelings. Do you? Say, "No".

ALIX "No."

ARBITER Then apologise for getting my hopes up. Say, "Sorry".

ALIX does not move.

ARBITER Say, "Sorry".

ALIX "Sorry."

ARBITER Thank you for compliance. Now, let's do some vitals before we get going on your little issue. Alix – it's very important you answer truthfully so that I get an accurate idea of your current state. Say, "I understand".

ALIX   Can I/

ARBITER   Say it.

ALIX   "I understand."

The ARBITER sits and begins ticking through his list of questions.

ARBITER   How are you feeling today? Say, "Never been better".

ALIX   "Never been better."

ARBITER   Any pain? Say, "No".

ALIX   "No."

ARBITER   Any fogginess? Say, "I don't think so".

ALIX   "I don't think so."

ARBITER   Not sure of fogginess? Suggests a little to me. That's understandable. Nod your head.

ALIX nods his head.

ARBITER   Any transgressions? Say, "Yes".

ALIX   But/

ARBITER   Say, "Yes". Comply.

ALIX   "Yes."

ARBITER   Touching yourself? Say, "Yes".

ALIX   "Yes."

ARBITER   And what have you been thinking about, when you've been playing with yourself like a little monkey all over the place? Say, "Men".

ALIX looks as though he might cry.

ARBITER   Alix... don't make things hard on yourself.

ALIX   Men.

ARBITER   Say, "Men", again.

ALIX   "Men. Men."

ARBITER   Okay, that's enough. We all get it. You don't need to rub it in our faces. Say, "Men" again.

ALIX   "Men."

ARBITER   And what is it about men that makes you touch yourself, Alix? Is it their bodies? Say, "Yes".

ALIX   "Yes."

ARBITER   With more feeling please.

ALIX   "Yes."

ARBITER   Are you thinking about men now? Say, "Yes".

ALIX   "Yes."

ARBITER   Are they naked? Say, "Yes".

ALIX   "Yes."

ARBITER   Even me?! Say, "Yes".

ALIX   "Yes."

ARBITER   Good grief. What a show. All things considered.

ALIX opens his mouth wide.

ARBITER   You wish to speak? Good Alix. You're getting it. And half of it, is getting it. Speak.

ALIX   Who are you?

ARBITER   I'm your Arbiter. All inductees are assigned an arbiter. You can call me Arb if you like, I don't mind that. Or you could call me bitter, I suppose. My wife would probably attest to that. *(Beat)* Laugh.

ALIX laughs meekly.

ARBITER   It was a trite joke but it deserved more than that. Laugh harder.

ALIX laughs harder.

ARBITER   Now you're just flattering me.

ALIX opens his mouth again.

ARBITER   Getting quite chatty, aren't you? Speak.

ALIX   What is an Arbiter?

ARBITER   I'll be a lot of things, Alix. But mostly, I'm here to help. You understand you're here to be corrected. And that any chance of your success on the outside relies on full participation in the programme. Including rigorous mental and physical correction. Say, "I understand".

ALIX   "I understand."

ARBITER   If you succeed, you'll return. If you fail, you'll be relocated to the Other Place, to live with all the others who have... failed.

ALIX opens his mouth wide.

ARBITER   The time for talking is over. I have to complete your induction, Alix. Besides which, you're probably here because that mouth of yours has been open a little too much, hasn't it? Close the mouth.

ALIX closes his mouth. The ARBITER puts his pen and note pad away, straightens himself and stands to the side. Alix looks confused and worried.

ARBITER   Alix, lay on the floor please. Do it now.

ALIX lays on the floor.

ARBITER   Arms by your side, there's a good lad.

ALIX puts his arms by his side.

ARBITER   Thank you for complying. You're going to be corrected now. Do you understand what that means? Say, "Yes".

ALIX looks confused and doesn't say anything.

ARBITER   Say, "Yes", Alix.

He does not reply. We can hear footsteps.

ARBITER   Alix, say, "Yes".

ALIX does not move. The footsteps gather in pace and double in size.

ARBITER   Comply, Alix. You're going to be corrected. You understand what that means, don't you? Say, "Yes".

The footsteps turn to running and double in size again.

ARBITER   SAY, "YES", I SAID.

Louder and louder like a stampede.

ARBITER   SAY "YES".

It is deafening and ALIX seems to be the only one registering the sound. ARB doesn't move.

ALIX   YES. YES. YES.

Suddenly silence, except for ALIX's heavy breathing.

ARBITER   Thank you for compliance. Welcome to
the programme.

ALIX cries out.

Blackout.

3

*Lights up on the Blue Room. ALIX is asleep on his bed.
He is beaten black and blue. Mostly around the head.
MARCUS sits on the edge of his bed staring at him for
some time. He also has cuts and bruises but they appear
to be less fresh. ALIX wakes suddenly, crying out.*

ALIX   What the fuck?

MARCUS   Don't worry, you're okay. I'm not an
Arbiter.

ALIX   Where am I?

MARCUS   In your room.

ALIX   Cell.

MARCUS   If the Arbiter hears you call it that,
you'll be corrected.

ALIX   How come you're speaking to me?

MARCUS   Why wouldn't I? *(Sarcastic)* You're my
new roomie, right?

ALIX   Fuck.

MARCUS   Got you bad?

ALIX   I don't understand why you're talking to me.

MARCUS   Fine. Suit yourself.

ALIX   I just mean... Won't you be... Corrected?

MARCUS   You're allowed to talk in your dorm. It's about the only place you are allowed.

ALIX   My head feels like it's been stamped on.

MARCUS   It probably has.

ALIX   Great.

MARCUS   Why are you in? I mean... I know why you're in... I just mean... you know... How?

ALIX   I don't want to talk about it.

MARCUS   That's fine. My last roomie was like that. They all talk in the end though. Gagging to talk.

ALIX   What happens now?

MARCUS   You wait. They'll probably let you recover a bit and then start correction again.

ALIX   I need to get out of here.

MARCUS   Not all correction is physical. You'll get through it. You have to. There's no way out.

ALIX   Figures.

MARCUS   You'll get used to it.

ALIX   How long have you been here?

MARCUS   I'm a bit confused on days and nights at the moment, they're trying to stop me counting.

ALIX   So you have no idea?

MARCUS Three months. No. Yeah. Three. I
think.

ALIX Jesus Christ.

MARCUS I'm pretty near to reintegration though.
My arbiter is confident I'll be out in time for Christmas.

ALIX It's June.

MARCUS Is it? I have it down as October. Nearly
Halloween.

ALIX It's June.

MARCUS Are you sure?

ALIX Yeah.

MARCUS Summer then. Nice.

ALIX You seem... happy. Are you happy...
here?

MARCUS I'm content.

ALIX Why *are* you here?

MARCUS Because I want to live. You should
sleep some more. You never know when they'll be back.

ALIX Yeah.

MARCUS It won't all be bad. I feel much better.
Trust it. Believe in it.

ALIX You're the first person here to be nice
to me.

MARCUS We're roomies. We need to look out
for each other. Having a roomie you can vent to and
get your frustration out with is part of the programme.
The dorms aren't bugged or anything – and it's better
to vent here than with the Arbiter.

ALIX   I don't think I can do this.

MARCUS   You haven't got a choice.

ALIX   I know.

Pause.

MARCUS   Do you want some help?

ALIX   What do you mean?

MARCUS   Here.

MARCUS moves over to ALIX. He places one hand on his chest/heart and the other on his back.

MARCUS   I can feel your pain. Your heart. *(As if talking to his heart)* Slow. Slow. Slow. That's better. It was fast. *(Pause)* Thank goodness you've come here. Welcome Alix. Welcome.

Blackout.

4

Lights up on the Red Room. The ARBITER is stood to one side of the table and ALIX is stood to the other side. ALIX stares out and the ARBITER stares at him.

ARBITER   You may sit.

ALIX sits.

ARBITER   Thank you for compliance. Do you mind if I sit? Say, "Not at all."

ALIX   "Not at all."

ARBITER   Too kind. So, today I'm afraid your head might get rather big, and not just because of the swelling. No, today I want to talk about you. I want to know why you think you're here and what you hope to get out of it. I'm also going to allow some free speech in this session, if that's okay with you. Say, "It's okay".

ALIX   "It's okay."

ARBITER   Good. You are now in free speech mode. Do you like it?

ALIX says nothing.

ARBITER   Do you like it?

ALIX   Yes.

ARBITER   Glad to hear it.

ALIX   So, I can speak whenever I want now?

ARBITER   Until I say you can't. But let's make this more interesting. Place both your palms on the table for me. Alix, this table can read your palms. It will record whether you lie to us or not.

ALIX   Will it hurt?

ARBITER   I don't think so. Then again, I've never done it. Pop your hands on there.

ALIX   Okay.

ALIX places his palms flat down on the table.

ARBITER   What's your father's name?

ALIX   John.

ARBITER   Do you love him?

ALIX   Yes.

ARBITER   And your mother?

ALIX   Grace, and yes, I love her.

ARBITER   Give it a chance, Alix.

ALIX   Sorry.

ARBITER   Do you think they're proud of you?

ALIX   What do you mean?

ARBITER   Don't ask questions. I'm the fucking Arbiter, not you.

ALIX   Yes.

ARBITER   "Yes what"?

ALIX   Yes, I think I've made them proud.

ARBITER   I didn't ask if you felt you had in the past. I asked if they were proud of you now.

ALIX   Probably not.

ARBITER   Why?

ALIX   Because of how I am.

ARBITER   And how are you?

ALIX   I'm fine, how are you?

The ARBITER laughs.

ARBITER   So, you're funny, are you?

ALIX   Sorry. I wasn't trying to be rude/

ARBITER   No offence taken, Alix. I just want to get to the truth because I don't think your parents are very proud of you, are they?

ALIX   Why would you say that?

ARBITER   Because you fuck men, don't you Alix?

ALIX   I wouldn't put it like that.

ARBITER   Where do you put it? We'd all like to
   know.

ALIX   I mean, I'd say that I fall in love with
   men.

ARBITER   Yes. I saw that in your notes. "Love."
   Do you think they would be proud of that?

ALIX   Of loving someone?

ARBITER   Of fucking a man.

ALIX   No, probably not.

ARBITER   Otherwise, they wouldn't have called
   the police, would they?

ALIX   No.

ARBITER   Your father thinks you're disgusting.
   "Ungodly" is the word I have.

ALIX   Is that right?

ARBITER   What it says here. He's a nice chap. I
   met him. He's not like you, is he?

ALIX   No.

ARBITER   What about Mummy? Has she told you
   how she feels about you?

ALIX   I know she loves me.

ARBITER   Um... no... that's not what I have.

ALIX   What you have is shit.

ARBITER   Now, we won't hurl insults, Alix. We
   won't do that.

ALIX   You're trying to break me.

ARBITER   Is it working?

ALIX   Yes.

ARBITER   Good. No... I have here that she thinks, and I quote, "They should all be locked up and sent straight to the Other Place". She doesn't even believe in correction.

ALIX   That's a lie.

ARBITER   It's not. She was on the BBC talking about it.

ALIX   What?

ARBITER   Yes. She believes that you're a "lost cause". That anybody who "does the things you have done is a lost cause and is unsalvageable." God, parents! They're awful, aren't they.

ALIX   Yes.

ARBITER   Not mine. Love 'em to bits. We still holiday together, you know. Extraordinary. They say some people tire of it but I wouldn't miss it for the world. But your parents... goodness. How could they have imagined their son would be such a disappointment?

ALIX   They love me.

ARBITER   This is why correction is so important. It's a very old notion, the idea that a parent's love is unconditional. Do you think your mother was proud of you when she found your internet search history? The pictures on your phone? Do you think she likes thinking of her little boy fucking men? You're disgusting.

ALIX   I'm not/

ARBITER   Free speech has ended. "I'm disgusting". Say it.

ALIX   "I'm disgusting."

ARBITER   "What I've done to my parents is unforgivable."

ALIX   "What I've done to my parents is unforgiveable."

ARBITER   "I have shamed everyone I know and everyone I know is ashamed of me."

ALIX   "I have shamed everyone I know and everyone I know is ashamed of me."

ARBITER   "I have broken the law."

ALIX   Your laws/

ARBITER   "I have broken the law/"

ALIX   "I have broken the law."

ARBITER   Alix, I know you're old enough to remember how it was in the before. But we don't live in the before anymore. This way is better. Your wife will thank you. Your children will thank you. You're going to be happy. Say, "Thank you for helping me."

ALIX   "Thank you for helping me."

ARBITER   You're very welcome. I think this is a break through. And so early on. Yes, I think minor corrections today. Would you agree. Say, "Yes. Thank you."

ALIX   "Yes. Thank you."

ARBITER   They will be pleased, I'm sure.

ALIX opens his mouth wide.

ARBITER   A question? Why not? Speak.

ALIX   Can I call my parents?

ARBITER   Why?

ALIX   Because I/

ARBITER   Best to think of your parents as dead now.

ALIX opens his mouth wide.

ARBITER   Chatty, chatty, chatty. Speak.

ALIX   Are they dead?

ARBITER   You know as well as I do I can't tell you anything. If you return you'll find out. Just think, if they're alive, what a nice surprise it will be.

ALIX opens his mouth again.

ARBITER   Last one.

ALIX   How long will I be here?

ARBITER   How long is a piece of string? You're free to leave to the Other Place whenever you wish. I'd stick it out if I were you. Lay on the floor.

ALIX lays on the floor with his mouth wide open.

ARBITER   Have a good week. Let's make it a month in fact.

Blackout.

5

Lights up on the Blue Room. ALIX is reading and MARCUS is writing in his journal.

ALIX   What are you writing?

MARCUS   Journal.

ALIX   How's that go? "Day 5000 – got

kicked… again". Careful how you write. A lot of good writers turned out to be poofy you know. Wouldn't want them to think you went backwards because you accidentally wrote a haiku.

MARCUS   You're so hung up on it all, aren't you?

ALIX   Aren't you?

MARCUS   Things change. You just need to get on with it.

ALIX   Yeah you're right. One day something's legal, the next illegal.

MARCUS   It's always been illegal.

ALIX   No it hasn't.

MARCUS   Yes it has. You just don't realise it. You'll get there.

ALIX   You're brainwashed. *(Pause)* What did you do? Before you came here?

MARCUS   I was a barman. Cocktail bar in Soho.

ALIX   That was one of the old gay districts.

MARCUS   There were no gay districts.

ALIX   What are you talking about?

MARCUS   Never mind.

ALIX   Do you miss it?

MARCUS   I miss people. Socialising.

ALIX   Yeah. Socialising. I get you.

MARCUS   I don't mean sex. I don't miss that.

ALIX   How can you not miss sex?

MARCUS   Too much effort.

ALIX   It shouldn't be.

MARCUS   If it's dissenting talk then I'll have to ignore you.

ALIX   We can talk in here. You said it yourself. They don't listen.

MARCUS   Not for them. For me. What don't you understand about the fact that I actually want to return? I don't want to go to the Other Place. I want a family and children and a normal life.

ALIX   That's a normal life, is it? You should be able to live as you. You can have a normal life.

MARCUS   Not if I keep talking about the old me, I can't. I want to get out. Don't you?

ALIX   Of here? Of course. But to go back. I don't know. Maybe I will go to the Other Place. If there's more people like us there, then why wouldn't I?

MARCUS   Then why don't you? You can go anytime...

ALIX   Because nobody knows anything about it and because once you go, you can't go back. I've got a family as well, you know.

MARCUS   Then give yourself up to it. It's the only way you'll get back. You're just a baby. You've only just started.

ALIX   I just don't believe you have accepted it.

MARCUS   Well, I have.

ALIX   So easily. Don't you miss holding his hand?

MARCUS   No, I don't. And neither should you.

ALIX   I miss him. I miss him so much.

MARCUS   Where is he?

ALIX   I don't know. They took him too.

MARCUS   You were caught.

ALIX   Yeah.

MARCUS   In the act?

ALIX   Not exactly. We were followed. They separated us and I haven't seen him since. The Arbiter won't tell me anything about him. He acts confused like I've made him up. Like he doesn't exist.

MARCUS   That correction is "invisibility". They'll acknowledge your wrongs and then right them by suggesting there never was an issue. That your condition never existed.

ALIX   That doesn't make any sense.

MARCUS   Imagine you could put all the bad things about you into a tiny box and put it at the back of your mind. Then imagine somebody tells you that actually that box never existed. That's what it is.

ALIX   So, in the end I'll say that *we* never existed?

MARCUS   What we felt... How we thought... Never existed. That's what I believe.

ALIX   So, if I tell you now, that what I felt with him, what we had, that it was wild and weird and wonderful and palpable and everything. That it was my life, that it consumed me. That it was love. You'd say/

MARCUS   It's all in your head. It never existed.

ALIX   Wow.

MARCUS   Obey the law. Embrace the right way. Release your shame. Be seen.

ALIX   And if I don't want to?

MARCUS   Go to the Other Place. With the rest.

ALIX   Right. And live with nothing.

MARCUS   You don't know that.

ALIX   It's bound to be. It's bound to be another prison or a ghetto. I've heard the rumours.

MARCUS   Then don't take the chance. Be seen.

ALIX   You tell me to be seen but to me you're the one that's invisible! *(Long pause)* How did they get you?

MARCUS   What do you mean?

ALIX   How did they catch you?

MARCUS   Oh, they didn't. I came voluntarily.

Blackout.

6

Lights up on the Red Room. The ARBITER is perched on the table. ALIX reads from a Bible. There are many books on the table. Piles and piles of them. Old and new, in all different shapes and sizes.

ARBITER   Alix. Free speech. Why are we here?

ALIX   You're opening a library.

ARBITER   Levity. Good. Try again.

ALIX   They're books.

ARBITER   What types of book?

ALIX   They look like religious ones.

ARBITER   Give him ten points. Yes – they are religious texts from all the major religions in the world. We're going to play a game.

ALIX   It's not Twister is it? I have a bad back from all the kicking.

ARBITER   Nobody likes a moaner. No, I'd like you to spend the afternoon going through these books and finding out where it says a man should lay with a man.

ALIX   It's pointless.

ARBITER   Ye of little faith.

ALIX   None of them will.

ARBITER   Really? Are you sure?

ALIX   Yes. I know what you're doing.

ARBITER   No you don't. You have no idea.

ALIX   None of them will say that. They'll probably say the opposite.

ARBITER   Why do you think that is?

ALIX   Because all religions are bigoted?

ARBITER   Are they?

ALIX   Their books are.

ARBITER   Nice correction.

ALIX   They'll say that laying with another man is wrong.

ARBITER   Just that?

ALIX   Any same sex.

ARBITER   And Others?

ALIX   LGBTQ+

ARBITER   Don't validate. We say Others.

ALIX   I am an "Other".

ARBITER   You won't be for long. Don't worry. Try not to worry.

ALIX   I'm not.

ARBITER   You are. You're worried. You're worried about what's inside these books. The truths.

ALIX   They can't all be true.

ARBITER   Some truths are universal.

ALIX   So, because not one of them specifically says that anything other than a heterosexual relationship is right, that makes it true.

ARBITER   What do you think?

ALIX   I think it's fucking bollocks.

ARBITER   And yet millions, billions of people believe them. Why do you think that is?

ALIX   They're brainwashed.

ARBITER   Make correction.

ALIX   They're misguided.

ARBITER   Could it be that they are right and you are the misguided one?

ALIX   Could be.

Pause.

ARBITER   What about Science, Alix?

ALIX I got a B at GCSE, is that any good to you?

ARBITER You should be a stand up. I'm talking more about that word "laying". There's no justification for it, is there? Scientifically?

ALIX Justification for what?

ARBITER Sticking your cock up another man's arse.

ALIX There is actually.

ARBITER Try me.

ALIX Love.

ARBITER Love is a cock in the arse?

ALIX That's not all love is but sex – the physicalising of how you feel – that's an expression of love.

ARBITER So, you *are* an academic?

ALIX Not everyone does that, anyway.

ARBITER Don't they?

ALIX It's pretty hard for a lesbian to do it.

ARBITER Yes, I suppose you're right. *(Long pause)* You're thinking about fucking a man right now, aren't you.

ALIX I'm thinking about loving a man.

ARBITER Answer. "I'm thinking about fucking a man right now".

ALIX I'm not.

ARBITER Answer. "I'm thinking about fucking a man right now."

ALIX I fucking hate you. I fucking hate you. I fucking hate you. I fucking hate you.

ALIX continues saying it. He is lost. He is tired. He is overwhelmed. He crawls under the desk, puts his hands over his ears, and curls up. The ARBITER continues shouting at him, hurling abuse, building to a crescendo.

ARBITER I can see we're done today. I'll see you in a few months. Here. Keep a book.

Blackout.

7

Lights up on the Blue Room. ALIX is on his own, laying on his bed. He is reading. He has been freshly beaten and his arm is in a sling.

After some time, we hear the sound of a large door, MARCUS is thrown in. He is covered in fresh blood. He cannot breathe and gets on all fours and breaths deeply. He gasps like a dying dog.

ALIX Oh my god, are you okay?

MARCUS *(barking explosively)* Get away from me.

ALIX But you/

MARCUS Don't touch me. Don't touch me. Don't touch me.

ALIX Okay, okay.

MARCUS Just give me a minute.

MARCUS continues the violent deep breaths trying to catch them. We can see the concentration in his face. He seems to be able to train himself to deal with the pain. To work through it. ALIX is mesmerised by him. Eventually, his breathing slows and he sits up. He is a bloody mess.

MARCUS   Towel.

ALIX   What/

MARCUS *(indicating the bed)* TOWEL.

ALIX rushes and gets the towel. MARCUS snatches it and dabs at his face.

ALIX   What happened?

MARCUS   What are you reading?

ALIX   It doesn't matter. What happened?!

MARCUS   Please... What are you reading?

ALIX *(Pause)*   The Gospel of John.

MARCUS   Any good?

ALIX   Lots of stuff about Jesus being bread.

MARCUS   I know it. "I am the bread from heaven."

ALIX   Yeah. Amazing that they've given me a book in which a man goes around asking people to eat him – couldn't be gayer could it?

MARCUS laughs and then winces.

ALIX   What happened?

MARCUS   God is good.

ALIX   Which one?

MARCUS   Any of them.

ALIX   I'm a cynic.

MARCUS   And yet, here you are, reading it.

ALIX   I don't have a choice. Besides which I'm not really reading it... I keep drifting off and thinking about Barbra Streisand.

MARCUS   Who's Barbra Streisand?

ALIX   Fuck. They really have wiped youO haven't they.

MARCUS   I'm struggling today. I... I...

He cannot finish his sentence.

ALIX   I didn't mean to upset you. I'm sorry.

MARCUS   I... can't... Hel/

ALIX   She's an icon.

MARCUS   Is she? I don't remember. I...

MARCUS really struggles – he is scared by his vagueness.

ALIX   It's Okay. *(Pause)* When I was about 18 I found these old CDs helping my mum clear out the loft. I asked her what they were and she said they probably had old music on and that they were useless now because nobody kept CD players anymore. On one was written 'Streisand in Concert'. There were some others as well: Oasis, Take That, The Verve but I kept the Streisand one because it had no case and was just tucked in behind a different one. I kept it and asked my music teacher at school about it and he went into the back cupboard and brought out this little CD Walkman thing and we played it and listened on one earphone each. She was amazing. Her voice just soared. I can remember the entire set list like it was yesterday – SOMETHING'S COMING, THE WAY WE WERE, CRY ME A RIVER, A SLEEPIN' BEE,

SOMETHING WONDERFUL, BEING ALIVE... HAPPY DAYS ARE HERE AGAIN. Every single line she sang I clung to. *(Sings with a fabulous impression)* *"So long... sad times... go long... bad times... we are rid of you at last..."* Beautiful.

MARCUS   Why was he showing you that? Your teacher? He shouldn't have been doing that.

ALIX   He knew how I was. He could tell I was different. Some teachers can.

MARCUS   Was he different?

ALIX   I think so. We never spoke about it. He helped me to understand though. It's so fucking impossible to know. No one talks about it. They just act like it doesn't exist.

MARCUS   Because it doesn't.

ALIX *(Beat)*   It took me listening to that voice singing to realise how profoundly unhappy I was and to do something about it. To try and be myself – and find others like me.

MARCUS   And did you?

ALIX   Yeah. Time goes on though and you get relaxed about it. My mum found the Walkman and the CD and... well... I was moved schools and it was all taken away. No more "Barbra Streisand Fan Club" in the old buildings abandoned toilets on Friday afternoons. Me, wearing a mop on my head and using the broom as a mic, standing on a shitty old toilet singing "Happy days are here again". Lip Syncing it with all of my soul. I want to say "it sounds stupid doesn't it" but I'd be saying that for you. It doesn't sound stupid to me. It's the only kind of real I've ever felt. It's when I fucking lived. I go there sometimes at night. When I close my eyes. Just for a moment. Do you ever have somewhere you go? To make it all go away?

Silence.

MARCUS   I need to sleep.

ALIX   Yeah.

MARCUS   It's late.

ALIX   Is it? *(Pause)* I wish I knew more about you.

MARCUS   Okay.

ALIX   I like you.

MARCUS   I like you.

ALIX   Then tell me something. Please.

MARCUS   It's not allowed.

ALIX   I know. But in here/

MARCUS   Can I have a hug?

ALIX is speechless.

MARCUS   Actually... never mind...

MARCUS lays down on the bed. He turns over. We hear him crying.

ALIX   Here.

ALIX puts the book down and slowly goes over to the bed. He lays his hand on MARCUS, who turns. ALIX stares at him and then hugs him.

MARCUS   Thank you.

Blackout.

8

Lights up on the Red Room. ALIX sits with head phones in. The ARBITER is sat opposite him. They stare at each other. We hear what ALIX is hearing in his ears. It is a recorded voice in the style of an educational tape.

RECORDED VOICE AIDS was a plague sent by God to end homosexuality because homosexuality is a sin.

AIDS was a plague sent by God to end homosexuality because homosexuality is a sin and is not part of the natural order, which is to say sex is between a man and a woman.

AIDS was a plague sent by God to end homosexuality because homosexuality is a sin and is not part of the natural order, which is to say sex is between a man and a woman. Only this sex can produce a baby which is the natural order.

AIDS was a plague sent by God to end homosexuality because homosexuality is a sin and is not part of the natural order, which is to say sex is between a man and a woman. Only this sex can produce a baby which is the natural order. Sodomy will never produce a baby. It's disgusting and you are disgusting. Your obsession with the rectum is disgusting. You can choose not to be disgusting. You can choose not to be homosexual.

AIDS was a plague sent by God to end homosexuality because homosexuality is a sin and is not part of the natural order, which is to say sex is between a man and a woman. Only this sex can produce a baby which is the natural order. Sodomy will never produce a baby. It's disgusting and you are disgusting. Your obsession with the rectum is disgusting. You can choose not to be disgusting. You can choose not to be homosexual. You can choose not to get AIDS and die.

End of Side One.

ARBITER   Play Side Two.

Blackout.

9

Lights up on the Blue Room. ALIX and MARCUS are cross legged on the floor. They are playing cards.

ALIX   Do you know 'Cheat'?

MARCUS   No.

ALIX   Some people call it 'Bullshit.'

MARCUS   No. I only know one game.

ALIX   'Rummy' is the most boring game. There's no flair. Nothing fruity in it.

MARCUS   Is that why you've lost ten hands in a row?

ALIX   Is it ten?

MARCUS   Yeah. You're really bad.

ALIX   Can we change? Please.

MARCUS   No. Just because you're losing. I like it.

ALIX   Maybe you can't change. Is that it? You used to know more, but then they wiped your mind?

Pause.

ALIX   That was a joke by the way.

MARCUS *(laughing a little)* Oh.

ALIX   I wish I'd known you before all this.

MARCUS   Do you?

ALIX   There's something I can't get past. Something they've taken. Isn't there?

MARCUS   I've always been like this.

ALIX   Like what?

MARCUS   Reserved.

ALIX   We've been here months. I feel like I don't know you at all.

MARCUS   It's your turn.

ALIX   Sorry.

They play.

MARCUS   What do you want to know?

ALIX   I don't know.

MARCUS   I don't mind you asking as long as you don't mind if I choose not to answer. They say I'm so close to getting out I don't want to jeopardise it.

ALIX   This is safe space though. We're allowed to do whatever we like in here.

MARCUS   I don't want it to influence me outside of the room. That's the test. The freedom to do as you please but to not act on it. That's the whole point.

ALIX   But what's the point of doing anything if it's not directly how you feel?

MARCUS   You wouldn't break the law just because you felt like it.

ALIX   Loving somebody shouldn't be against the law.

MARCUS   It isn't.

ALIX   But it is.

MARCUS   Lots of people get by *not* acting on it.

ALIX   That's not official policy.

MARCUS   I know but not everyone needs correction. They can be corrected by themselves. Making little corrections all the time. Do you not understand that?

ALIX   I think what's natural is natural. Choice is a fallacy. A denial.

MARCUS   Think of it like this: a child goes to a... sweet shop and he sees the things he wants – his eyes tell him they look tasty, his nose can smell the sugar, his fingers tingle with the prospect of holding it, his tongue with tasting it but in his hand is a 50 pence piece and these things he wants, right, these things he wants are on the top shelf, they cost a pound... does he steal them? His senses are triggered at the prospect of them, that's natural... maybe... but that doesn't mean he is entitled to them... it isn't the natural progression and development of the moment that he should have them... to take is not the natural order... he makes a choice.

ALIX   You sound like an Arbiter.

MARCUS   So, you think it's okay to steal it? To take?

ALIX   Not if it's a *Bounty*, I don't like coconut.

MARCUS   I can't talk to you.

ALIX   My point is we're not talking about sweets are we?

MARCUS   It's like Eve.

ALIX   Oh Jesus.

MARCUS   She had a choice.

ALIX   What choice? He made *her,* He made the garden and then He put the fucking snake there! Some choice.

MARCUS   You don't get it.

ALIX   I understand the words. I don't understand why.

MARCUS   I want to go back. That's why I'm trying.

ALIX   It's been months and every two weeks you tell me they've told you you're only weeks, sometimes days, from going back though. Why do you trust them?

MARCUS   What else do we have?

ALIX   We have each other.

MARCUS   Do we?

ALIX   I liked holding you.

MARCUS   That's fine.

ALIX   No... I mean... I wanted to/

MARCUS   If you're going to talk to me like that then/

ALIX   Okay I'm sorry. I just... It's just... without you I think I'd have died in here. You're the only thing I look forward to. Just having somebody to talk to and who I know deep down is like me.

MARCUS   Am I?

ALIX   I think so. All we have is each other. We never see another soul. We might be the only two people in this whole place. The whole time I've been here I've only ever seen the Arbiter and you. Even the beatings are in the dark.

MARCUS   Corrections.

ALIX   Corrections, yeah. *(Pause)* What if we're the only ones in here? Maybe we should try and get out. Marcus? If I could get you out, would you go with me? *(Pause)* Marcus?

MARCUS   You're holding up the game.

ALIX realises he has won the game.

ALIX   Shit, I've won.

MARCUS   That's impossible.

ALIX   First time for everything.

MARCUS   You cheated, you must have.

ALIX   I didn't, okay. Jesus chill out, it's just a game.

MARCUS   Yeah, and I don't like cheaters.

ALIX   What is wrong with you?

MARCUS   What is wrong with me?! What is wrong with you?!

ALIX   Why are you shouting?

MARCUS   One pack of cards. We get one fucking pack of cards and just when I'm on a winning streak you fucking cheat. Is that what you're like on the outside?

ALIX   What?

MARCUS   One friend in the world and you treat them like that?

ALIX   Marcus, I/

MARCUS *(pushing ALIX aggressively)* Just fuck off, will you?

ALIX   Don't push me.

MARCUS walks away.

ALIX   Here have your cards, you baby.

ALIX, raging now, takes the cards and throws them at MARCUS. MARCUS turns and runs at ALIX and they squabble on ALIX'S bed. Eventually, they come to a point where both have each other in a stronghold unable to move and are staring at each other. They hold for a moment and then ALIX kisses MARCUS. MARCUS pulls away, eventually.

MARCUS   What are you doing?

ALIX   Don't you miss it?

ALIX kisses him again but this time MARCUS pulls away quickly.

MARCUS   What are you doing?

ALIX   I miss it in my soul.

MARCUS *(with great threat)* Get away from me.

MARCUS pushes ALIX down, gets off his bed and moves to his side of the room and turns with menace.

ALIX   Marcus, I/

MARCUS   Stay there. *(Beat)* Forever.

MARCUS gets into bed, turns over and goes to sleep. ALIX sits up in his bed. He stares at MARCUS. He struggles to hold back tears.

ALIX   I'm sorry.

Blackout.

End of Part One.

PART TWO

10

Lights up on the Red Room. ALIX is stood facing the back. He is naked with his trousers and pants around his ankles. His top is folded neatly on the table. We can see a wire is coming from him. He is bruised all over with deep welts in his back. The ARBITER stands upstage and looks at him. Behind him, on the back wall, is a white screen.

ARBITER   Are you feeling comfortable? You can speak freely.

ALIX   I have a wire wrapped around my cock, exactly how comfortable am I meant to be?

ARBITER   Today is an important day in your correction. The outcome of this test will give us a good idea of the progress you're making and whether or not we need extended measures.

ALIX   All a bit *Clockwork Orange,* isn't it?

ARBITER   I don't care for chocolate.

ALIX   That's chocolate orange. I said clockwork.

ARBITER   What is that?

ALIX   It's a film. It was a film.

ARBITER   I haven't seen it. I don't care for the arts. Cinema, theatre, music. All a bit subjective. I like to know where I stand.

ALIX   You don't like opinions.

ARBITER   I like opinions based on facts.

ALIX   Based on your facts. Based on your interpretation of your facts.

ARBITER   You can have your own opinions. You cannot have your own facts.

ALIX   But you can exclude facts to suit the facts you present.

ARBITER   Give me an example?

ALIX   Only heterosexual sex is valid because when men and women have sex it produces a baby.

ARBITER   That's true.

ALIX   Using only that fact on its own excludes all other views. It suggests that all other considerations aren't valid.

ARBITER   Why does it?

ALIX   Because just speaking it matters.

ARBITER   What other consideration should we be acknowledging in this scenario?

ALIX   I dunno... That fucking a guy in the arse is fucking amazing.

Silence.

ARBITER   Shall we press on? We have a lot to get through.

ALIX   Do what you want.

ARBITER   We're going to show you some material now and measure your responses to see if we're making any progress.

ALIX   How will you know?

ARBITER   If you make progress while you're

watching, so to speak, then we'll have made no progress.

ALIX   You're going to see if I get hard and
cum all over the place?

ARBITER   You can choose vulgarity if you so
wish. The film is three minutes. More than enough to
measure your development.

*The film is played. ALIX can see it on the back wall but all
the audience see is a white screen. Everything else is in
the imagination. This should be pretty explicit. The entire
thing plays. It is funny, disgusting, uncomfortable and
unbearable all at the same time.*

The tape ends.

ARBITER   The sequence has ended. You can
relax.

ALIX   Relax? I'm fucking horny as hell.

ARBITER   Get dressed.

*ALIX pulls up his pants and puts his top on. The ARBITER'S
demeanour has changed.*

ALIX   Do you mind leaving the room so I can
have a wank? *(He laughs)* Oi... I'm talking to you.

ARBITER   Without permission.

ALIX   I'm sorry. I said I'm sorry. Do you
think I could/

ARBITER   Now, is a time to be silent.

ALIX opens his mouth to speak.

ARBITER   Stop requesting.

ALIX closes his mouth.

ARBITER   Thank you. We will wait for the results. They should be relatively quick.

The ARBITER finishes some paperwork, fixes himself and then sits.

ARBITER   Perhaps you might use this time to think about your parents or your former family. About how you'd like to get back to them. About how they feel about what you've done. What you are. Who you have become. Perhaps you'd like to take some time to think about the hurt you've caused. The pain. This never-ending need and necessity to be different to everyone else. This overwhelming, almost inevitable obsession you have with being the centre of attention. Perhaps you might take this time to think about your former friends, those at school. The ones that used to like you. The ones that despised you. Perhaps you should think about the bus drivers, the teachers, the ticket takers, the dog walkers, the young children in the park, the dogs and cats, all the creatures of the earth that could smell it on you. Perhaps you might take this time. This small ounce of time. This modicum of time to think about all that and how it might all go away through your actions and your resolve and your will power and your conformity and your successes and your principles. Perhaps you should think about that.

A light bulb smashes.

ARBITER   Your results are ready.

ARB moves to the door and is handed a piece of paper. He reads through it silently. He sighs and looks at ALIX. ALIX stares at him.

ARBITER   Okay. Alix blink when you understand

me. You may blink now to say you understand that.

ALIX blinks.

ARBITER   Good. Now, it will be no surprise to you that you have failed this test.

ALIX blinks.

ARBITER   I'm sure you've also noticed by now but the wiring on you is not just for the test but also for control, and you cannot move now, can you?

ALIX blinks.

ARBITER   Other than to blink, of course.

ALIX blinks.

ARBITER   The system, Alix, has placed you in a paralysed state in order that we treat you. For you to move forward in the programme you must be treated and it's easier if you're completely still. The treatment is very effective in getting to the root of a patient's condition. Especially one as severe as yours. Does that make sense?

ALIX blinks.

ARBITER   Of course, all treatments are voluntary, just as this programme is voluntary. We wouldn't undertake it without your express permission. Please blink to say you understand and that you're happy for me to continue.

Pause.

ARBITER   Please give consent, Alix.

Pause.

ARBITER   Please blink.

Pause.

ARBITER   Please blink now.

ALIX holds his eyes open for as long as he can as the ARBITER continues to press him to blink. ALIX tries his best not to but eventually he has to blink.

ALIX blinks.

The ARBITER blinds him.

ARBITER   Thank you.

Blackout.

11

Lights up on the Blue Room. ALIX is curled up on his bed with his back to the audience and MARCUS. MARCUS sits and stares at him. He gets up slowly and walks over to ALIX and sits on the edge of his bed.

MARCUS   Are you okay? *(Pause)* Will you let me see? *(Long pause)* I have a sister. Had one. I haven't seen her in three years. She'll be nineteen now. Just going off to university. She always knew. When she was younger, I used to take her down the park and play with her... down the slide, on the swings. As she got older, she realised part of it was because I just wanted to spy on the footballers across the field. She wasn't stupid. She didn't mind. Eventually, our park trips would turn into bench sits with some food and some music. She'd ask me lots of questions. She had no idea. Nobody speaks about it. It's like it doesn't exist. She was so smart for her age. A fourteen-year-old telling me that it's okay to feel the way I do and that "Mum and Dad love each other so what's the difference?" Later that year she told me I should talk to this one boy who never seemed to play and was always on the subs bench and so eventually I did. *(Pause)* Then I started seeing him more often. Soon the park trips turned into a good excuse to go out to meet him. She'd happily sit on her phone while we went for a walk. Just to get out of sight. Just to hold each other. Every time I came back, I'd be beaming and she'd beam for me. Ask me all about him. He was built like a footballer but he obviously couldn't play. Tall and slim with a tan. Must have been all the sitting in the bench in the sun. I can still feel how tightly he used to hold me and how he smelt. Too much deodorant.

Eventually, we snuck out one night and I met him in the woods just off the park. He'd laid out this blanket and brought these candles. When I got there and he surprised me, he looked so vulnerable. This big footballer was totally in love with me. Madly in love with me. And I was with him. It was the best night of my life. Sometimes when I know they're not listening – I relive it. Just for a moment. When it matters. Then a couple of weeks later I came home and these men were waiting. My mum was so still, she didn't move or look at me. My dad was crying. And my sister was in the doorway. She just stared at me. I never realised they had their suspicions and were using her to catch us. When I looked at her... When I looked at her to ask why, she told me they'd shown her a video on why they do what they do. You probably remember the one and that what we were doing was sick and against the... well, you know all that.

I never saw him again and they brought me straight here. I can still see that thirteen-year-old girl, excited to hear about my day though. And that man who I never saw again. *(Pause)* Now, you know about me.

ALIX turns over.

ALIX   Thank you.

MARCUS   Oh. They've blinded you.

ALIX cries. MARCUS strokes ALIX.

Blackout.

12

Lights up on the Red Room. ALIX sits at a table. He is alone. He waits. He is visibly broken. He sits desperately alone for some time. Eventually the ARBITER enters with a spring in his step.

ARBITER   Another day, another... Free speech. How are you finding it?

ALIX   Finding what?

ARBITER   Life without your eyes.

ALIX   I/

ARBITER   Let's get on, shall we.

ALIX   Yes.

ARBITER   Alix, I'm going to ask you a series of questions today. I want us to acknowledge your transgressions and to face them. Head on.

ALIX   Okay.

ARBITER   Are you frightened?

ALIX   No.

ARBITER   Yes, you are. It's okay to be frightened. It's not every day we face ourselves. Fully face ourselves. The greater privilege for you is your ability now to be inward looking. To face things without seeing them.

ALIX   You want me to imagine myself better.

ARBITER   On the contrary. I want you to face yourself free of distraction. Focused. Determined.

ALIX   Whatever you want, I'll do.

ARBITER   I know. Face me. Place both your palms on the table and focus on what I say to you.

ALIX does as he says.

ARBITER   Answer quickly. Answer concisely. Give me no more information than I ask for. Do you understand?

ALIX   I can't move my hands. My hands are stuck.

ARBITER   Alix, calm down. There are always measures. Do as I say and you'll be fine. Progress can be made. I believe in you.

ALIX   Please.

ALIX starts to cry.

ARBITER   Concentrate.

ALIX   I want my mummy.

ARBITER   Recall the colour of the sky.

ALIX *(calling out)* Mum!

ARBITER *(like a military general)* Concentrate now.

ALIX	I want to go home.
ARBITER	Recall the colour of the sky.
ALIX	Blue.
ARBITER	Good. Recall the colour of the sea.
ALIX	Blue.
ARBITER	Good. Recall the difference between the two.
ALIX	One is deeper.
ARBITER	Which?
ALIX	The sea. The water is darker.
ARBITER	Why darker?
ALIX	You can't see what's underneath. In the depths.
ARBITER	Good. Thank you for compliance. You see really this is about making you speak as clearly and honestly as possible. Getting to the route of how you perceive things; your actions. Let's continue. Recall a person.
ALIX	My mother.
ARBITER	Why not? Recall her eyes.
ALIX	Blue. No, brown. I... I can't remember.
ARBITER	That's good. Progress.
ALIX	I can't remember my mother's eyes. How long have I been here?
ARBITER	Good question. What day is it?
ALIX	Monday.
ARBITER	Guess again.

ALIX	Tuesday.
ARBITER	Guess again.
ALIX	I don't know.
ARBITER	Good. Recall another person.
ALIX	My father.
ARBITER	How tall is he?
ALIX	Six foot two.
ARBITER	Recall his smell.
ALIX	Musty. Old aftershave.
ARBITER	Recall his look.
ALIX	Stern. He looked through you.
ARBITER love more?	Recall your parents now. Who do you
ALIX	What?
ARBITER	You heard me Alix.
ALIX	My mother.
ARBITER	Why?
ALIX	She protected me.
ARBITER	What from?
ALIX	Transgressions.
ARBITER	Be specific.
ALIX	Fucking.
ARBITER	Perhaps a little much.
ALIX	My nature then.

ALIX is given an electric shock. He winces.

ARBITER   That is your first shock.

ALIX   It hurts. Fuck.

ARBITER   Of course, it does. It's designed to.

ALIX   Why?

ARBITER   You spoke a falsehood. It's not your "nature". That's not a word we use here. You know that. We must now start again.

ALIX   She caught me with/

ARBITER   It's of no consequence. We must start again. Forget it.

ALIX   I want to remember him.

ALIX is shocked again.

ARBITER   Forget. Recall a secret.

ALIX   I hit a boy.

ARBITER   Good. Recall another.

ALIX   I stole five pounds from my best friend.

ARBITER   Recall this friend.

ALIX   Her name was Tasha.

ARBITER   Good. Recall her reaction when she found out you stole from her.

ALIX   She was upset. Betrayed.

ARBITER   Recall another time you betrayed someone.

ALIX   I can't.

ALIX is shocked.

ALIX   Fuck!

ARBITER   Recall another time you betrayed someone.

ALIX   My brother.

ARBITER   What did you do?

ALIX   I told on him.

ARBITER   What did you tell?

ALIX   He was with a girl he shouldn't have been.

ARBITER   Why?

ALIX   She was much younger than him.

ARBITER   How young?

ALIX   She was underage.

ARBITER   How old?

ALIX   Fifteen.

ARBITER   How old was he?

ALIX   Nineteen.

ARBITER   How old were you?

ALIX   Twelve.

ARBITER   How did you find out?

ALIX   I saw them.

ARBITER   Where did you see them?

ALIX   Through the keyhole.

ARBITER   What were you doing?

ALIX   I was watching them.

ALIX is shocked. He wimpers.

ALIX	I was spying on them.
ARBITER	What did you see?
ALIX	They were messing around.
ARBITER	Recall what happened next.
ALIX	They were touching.
ARBITER	Recall where he touched her.
ALIX	Between her legs.
ARBITER	In her cunt, yes. Recall what happened next.
ALIX	She gasped.
ARBITER	It was nice, yes. Recall what happened next.
ALIX	They fucked on the bed.
ARBITER	You watched the whole thing, didn't you?
ALIX	Yes.
ARBITER	You pulled at yourself, didn't you?
ALIX	No.

ALIX is shocked. He moans.

ARBITER	Try again.
ALIX	I didn't.

ALIX is shocked again. He moans.

ALIX	They're getting more painful.
ARBITER	Try again.

ALIX	I tried to. I was confused.
ARBITER	What happened next?
ALI	I got frustrated and angry and ran and told my parents.
ARBITER	How did that make you feel?
ALIX	Worthless.
ARBITER	Like you betrayed him?
ALIX	Yes.
ARBITER	Like he trusted you?
ALIX	Yes.
ARBITER	And you betrayed him?
ALIX	Yes.
ARBITER	Like you did to your mummy.
ALIX	What?
ARBITER	Recall the time in your form room.
ALIX	How do you know about that?
ARBITER	Recall it.
ALIX	I won't.

ALIX is shocked. This is one of the worst he has felt. He yelps like a dog.

ARBITER   Alix, if you want to get through this then you need to play ball.

ALIX   I won't let you take everything.

ALIX is shocked. He moans.

ARBITER   Recall the time in your form room.

ALIX   No.

ALIX is shocked again. He cries out.

ARBITER   Alix, there comes a time in everyone's life when they must make a choice. A choice about who we want to be and what we want to do with the time we've been so graciously given. A defining choice. The ultimate choice. You however, at this particular moment in time, you stand on the precipice of a more immediate and simpler choice. Right here and now, you face the choice between walking out the door in the next five minutes alive or being carried out like just another fucking dead faggot.

ALIX   Cunt.

ARBITER   Fine. Double shock.

ALIX is shocked twice. Writhing in pain.

ALIX   I want my mummy.

ARBITER   She can't help you here. Only you can help yourself. What happened in the form room?

ALIX   Please.

ARBITER   Again.

ALIX is shocked twice.

ARBITER   You know I had a boy like you. Bigger though. Much bigger. Left here singed from head to toe. His eye balls popping out his brain. Again.

ALIX is shocked twice. He screams.

ARBITER   Again/

ALIX   We were talking.

ARBITER	Who is we?
ALIX	Me and my teacher.
ARBITER	Good. Recall his name.
ALIX	Mr. Shauneson.
ARBITER	Recall him.
ALIX	Kind.
ARBITER	Recall his features.
ALIX	Why do you have to take everything?
ARBITER	Double shock.

ALIX is shocked twice again.

ARBITER	Recall his features.
ALIX	Tall. Broad. Dark. Sexy as fuck.
ARBITER	Good.
ALIX	I don't get shocked for that.
ARBITER	Honesty is never shocked.
ALIX	Get fucked.

ALIX is shocked.

ALIX	I was being honest.
ARBITER	Vulgarity in dissemblance will be shocked. What were you doing with this teacher?
ALIX	Talking.
ARBITER	Recall what else.
ALIX	Playing music.
ARBITER	Recall what else.

ALIX	Reading.
ARBITER	Do not distract. Recall what else.
ALIX	I kissed him.
ARBITER	Recall what happened next.
ALIX	He kissed me back.
ARBITER	Recall what happened next.
ALIX	My mum walked in.
ARBITER	Recall her face.
ALIX	She was shocked.
ARBITER	Recall what she said.
ALIX	She called me a faggot.
ARBITER	Recall what happened next.
ALIX	She started hitting me and shouting at Mr. Shauneson.
ARBITER	Recall how she felt.
ALIX	I don't fucking know how she felt.

ALIX is shocked.

ALIX *(calling out)* Mum!

ARBITER	Recall how she felt.
ALIX	How can I know?
ARBITER	You can estimate from her expression.
ALIX	She was hurt.
ARBITER	Hurt that her son was a faggot?
ALIX	Yes.
ARBITER	Hurt that the one son she trusted

should betray her. She felt utterly disgusted by you, didn't she?

ALIX   Yes.

ARBITER   Recall what you did?

ALIX   I screamed and cried.

ARBITER   Did you want to die?

ALIX   I don't know.

ALIX is shocked.

ALIX   Yes.

ARBITER   Recall what the teacher did.

ALIX   He apologised and took the blame.

ARBITER   Recall how that made you feel.

ALIX   Like dying.

ARBITER   Recall what happened.

ALIX   Mum took me home and said nothing.

ARBITER   Recall what happened to the teacher.

ALIX   I never saw him again. Nobody did.

ARBITER   Where do you think he is?

ALIX   Somewhere here.

ALIX is shocked.

ARBITER   You're lying. It can tell. Where do you
think he is?

ALIX   The Other Place.

ARBITER   Thank you Alix. You can remove your
hands now.

ALIX does as quickly as possible. He immediately cowers in the corner. He is visibly shaking in pain, upset and terrified. He whimpers. The ARBITER moves to him and takes him in his arms, he wipes his brow with a tissue.

ARBITER   Alix. These sessions are important. I want you to know that your actions have consequences. You hurt people by what you do.

ALIX   I didn't hurt anybody.

ARBITER   Sorry.

ALIX   I didn't hurt anybody.

ARBITER   You hurt your mother.

ALIX   She's meant to love me.

ARBITER   And the teacher? That was appropriate?

ALIX   I was 18. In my last year. He was 22 for fuck's sake.

ARBITER   You may justify it how you wish/

ALIX   We found each other in hell. You wouldn't understand that.

ARBITER   I don't suppose I would. And the kiss?

ALIX   I wanted to know what it was like.

ARBITER   What?

ALIX   To love somebody and to realise it.

ARBITER   You mean you wanted to fuck him.

ALIX   You're obsessed with sex. It's all you ever talk about. Is that what you guys do?

ARBITER   Enlighten me.

ALIX   You sit around all day – telling us/

ARBITER   Us?

ALIX   People like me... Telling us to tell you everything about our lives. You drain us of everything, every tiny detail so you can take it home and use it.

ARBITER   I don't know what you mean.

ALIX   Are you gay?

Silence.

ARBITER   What did you say?

ALIX   Are you gay?

Silence.

ARBITER   In my experience, the greatest gift of progress is the period of reflection after. Try to reflect better.

ARBITER continues to wipe his brow.

ALIX *(quietly and inches from the ABRITER'S face)* You know, in my experience, people so opposed to something... people who have something so engrained often turn out to be big fat raging homos themselves.

ALIX takes the ARBITER'S face in both hands and gently kisses him. The ARBITER does not resist. It lasts more than a moment. As the ARBITER pulls away, he stares wide-eyed at ALIX. ALIX starts to laugh.

ALIX   You want to fuck me, don't you? That's what it is.

The ARBITER gets up and moves towards the door.

ALIX   Where are you going? *(ALIX gets to his feet, a broken shell of a human)* I know you. You want to put me on this counter don't you... I know. You want to take down my trousers and teach me a lesson. Show me how it's done. "You don't fuck a man like this, you fuck him like this."

The ARBITER doesn't move for a second. He breathes deeply.

ALIX   I can hear your breath. I can hear how deeply you're breathing. If you want it then take it. Come on.

The ARBITER looks around and moves towards him. He takes ALIX's face into his hands.

ALIX   Please. Take it. *(Pause)* Take it. *(The ARBITER stares at him)* Take it... and then admit what a screaming fucking hypocrite cunt you are.

The ARBITER moves his hands from ALIX'S face to his neck and begins to strangle him. ALIX fights back but the ARBITER is too strong and turns ALIX around and bends him over the table. The ARBITER starts to undo his trousers.

ALIX *(Shouts)* Marcus!

A bomb hits the facility.

ALIX is alone amongst the debris and across from him is the ARBITER – dead on the ground on his back. A faint siren can be heard as well as falling debris. ALIX crawls around – as he does the ARBITER'S monologue from earlier plays with echo, reverb and heavy bass on it. It is disorientating for ALIX who is trying to find his way around the stage.

ARBITER *(Recorded Voice)* Perhaps you might use this time to think about your parents or your former friends. About how you'd like to get back to them. About how they feel about what you've done. What you are. Who you have become. Perhaps you'd like to take some time to think about the hurt you've caused. The pain. This never-ending need and necessity to be different to everyone else. This overwhelming, almost inevitable obsession you have with being the centre of attention. Perhaps you might take this time. This small ounce of time. This modicum of time to think about all that and how it might all go away through your actions and your resolve and your will power and your conformity and your successes and your principles. Perhaps you should think about that.

ALIX finds the ARBITER and begins to feel up and down him. He feels for his pulse and then starts laughing. He begins to pound on his chest frantically. The entire facility is crumbling around him with all the systems failing.

ALIX   I fucking hate you.

I fucking hate you.
I fucking hate you.
I hate you.
I hate you.
I hate you.
I hate you.
I hate you.
I hate you.
I hate you.
I hate you.
I hate you.
I hate you.
I hate you.
I hate you.

Suddenly, the broken screen behind ALIX lights up and an educational video starts up.

ARBITER *(Recorded Video)* Sometimes what we see is painful. What we experience worse. You are sat here observing something that even you may feel uncomfortable with. But our history is a tawdry little affair. We musn't forget. It's true that in early medieval years, this condition was given no particular penance. It was viewed like all sins but as time moves on we find these acts, these perversions, undergo greater punishments. In thirteenth century France, conditional acts between men were frequently punished with castration for a first offence, dismemberment on the second, and burning alive on the third. In Italy, sodomy was punished with the confiscation of the offender's property by the authorities, and by 1553, Henry VIII – if some of you can remember that far back – decreed the death penalty would be used against those who committed single sex sodomy, in his rather jolly title: Buggery Act 1553. Now, the naysayers may decry this as primitive. So let's fast forward.

In the colonial era, Australia passed laws against the condition, again making it punishable by death and in the early 20th century these poor people were taken to camps and routinely tortured and tested on – like animals. And it goes on – in Sudan, punishment of one hundred lashes, in Iran, public hanging, in Cameroon corrective rape, in Chechnya, beatings. What do all these have in common? I'll tell you. Their ineffectiveness. They do not get to the route of the condition. They do not accept that the occupant is sick, or deluded. That they may be made better, should they so wish.

The work we do here is treatment. Conversion is the only sensible and effective way of treating the condition.

Are the methods invasive? Yes. So is the condition. Are the methods extreme? Yes. So is the condition. What you must ask yourself is, who would want to live in a society that treats a condition so poorly?

With deep echoes, we hear ALIX'S voice calling out "I want. I want."

ARBITER   Nobody would want this.

ALIX'S calling continues.

ARBITER   And those who say they do... the delusion and the condition are so ingrained, they very well may be, beyond hope. Their grasp on reality may be lost. But we don't give up. We try.

ALIX'S calling grows.

ARBITER   Unlike the societies of the past. We try. We give them the opportunity to fight. To fight their urge. To fight their circumstance. To challenge this reality.

ALIX'S calling continues.

ARBITER   We try. We try. We try.

ALIX'S calling melts into the scene and as the ARBITER leaves, we see ALIX amongst the debris of the Blue Room. Alone and curled up in a corner, he sobs and whimpers. He is blind and bloody.

MARCUS   Alix?

MARCUS appears at the side.

MARCUS   You survived.

ALIX   Am I dead?

MARCUS	You look alive to me.
ALIX	I think I'm dead.
MARCUS	I can feel your heart. You're alive.
ALIX	How did you survive? Are they all dead? What happened?
MARCUS	I don't know but there's a hole blown through the whole thing.
ALIX	I can't breathe.
MARCUS	Listen, we can get out. If you want to. We can go.
ALIX	What? To where?
MARCUS	Back.
ALIX	What if we're caught?
MARCUS	I think they're all dead.
ALIX	Is he?
MARCUS	I think so.
ALIX	Because they'll come back. They'll take more.
MARCUS	This is your only chance.
ALIX	You came back for me?
MARCUS	Of course.
ALIX	Why?
MARCUS	I care about you. You know that.

ALIX touches for MARCUS' face.

ALIX	You're hurt.
MARCUS	Not really.

ALIX   How did you/

MARCUS   All the systems went down.

ALIX   I haven't heard anything. It's just been
silent.

MARCUS   You won't.

ALIX feels down to his lips.

ALIX   I missed you.

MARCUS   I missed you.

ALIX   I want to kiss you.

MARCUS   Kiss me.

They kiss passionately.

ALIX   I've wanted that for so long.

MARCUS   Me too.

ALIX   It only took them to blind me and for a
bomb to hit the facility for you to realise.

MARCUS   You're so strong. This is my fault.

ALIX   How could this be your fault?

MARCUS   I should have tried to get us out when I
had the chance.

ALIX   You said yourself they could reverse
the treatment. Maybe if we stay, they'll see it as a good
thing and go easy on us.

MARCUS   You want to stay?

ALIX   But if we're caught.

MARCUS   You're ready to convert?

ALIX   Maybe I already have.

MARCUS   Then you should stay.

ALIX   I want to be with you.

MARCUS   Then come with me.

ALIX   I'm scared.

MARCUS   We won't survive in here.

ALIX   What about the Other Place?

MARCUS   What? With no food? Living on the streets? Begging? They might be slaves.

ALIX   They might not. Imagine if it's just a place for us. With people like us. A big fuck-off party with none of this shit.

MARCUS   When I first came here, I was in a room with another boy. He was like you.

ALIX   You never said.

MARCUS   It was too painful. We came in together. He fought the whole time like you. And they did exactly what they've done to you to him.

ALIX   You spent months telling me I was wrong.

MARCUS   I was afraid. I want to get out of here. I want to see my family.

ALIX   What happened to him?

MARCUS   They took him to the Other Place. My Arbiter used to tell me how much he was struggling. How they lived daily lives of pain and torment – knowing they'll never get back.

ALIX   He could be lying.

MARCUS   Why?

ALIX   To get you to do what he wants.

MARCUS   Arbiters don't lie. They're clinical. It's part of the oath they take.

ALIX   So you believed him and/

MARCUS   Committed to conversion.

ALIX   So, what's changed? Why do you want to go now?

MARCUS   You. I didn't feel about him like I feel about you.

ALIX feels for MARCUS' face again.

ALIX   I have to kiss you again.

They kiss.

MARCUS   I'll follow you. Whatever you want to do. It's your choice. We can stay or we can go.

ALIX   One night.

They kiss again.

MARCUS   One night.

ALIX   One night and then we can go. I promise.

MARCUS   Are you sure?

ALIX   Just one night.

They kiss again.

MARCUS   Your choice.

ALIX   Just one more night. Please. Hold me.

ALIX wraps MARCUS' arms around him. They kiss

passionately as sounds of debris fall about them. Suddenly, a loud siren can be heard. The sound comes over the speaker system, "System rebooting" ... it can clearly be heard failing... "This is a test. This is a test." The sounds short out to white noise and suddenly "Ave Maria" sung by Barbra Streisand begins to play, as if from an old record player. Another explosion. The lights short out and ALIX and MARCUS can only be seen in dark half-light. As the debris falls all about them, they pull blankets over them so only the tops of their bodies can be seen in half-light. MARCUS takes ALIX'S top off revealing the extent of his pain. ALIX cries as MARCUS kisses the marks on his neck and chest. ALIX takes MARCUS' top off and returns the gesture. They kill the violence with their love. They start to kiss more passionately and as they lay down, they pull the covers over themselves so only their faces can be seen in deep red half-light. They make love.

The lights change with flashes and the sounds of debris grow over the music, including rumbling and sirens. As the music ends, the lights fade to black.

13

Lights up on the Red Room. It is, as it was before the bomb, with no evidence of debris or destruction. MARCUS is gone. The ARBITER stands over ALIX who lays crumpled on the floor in only his underwear.

ARBITER	Get up.
ALIX	Marcus...
ARBITER	Get up Alix.
ALIX	I thought you were dead.

ARBITER	I was for a moment.
ALIX	I felt you. I felt your pulse. You were dead.
ARBITER	Perception is a fickle thing. Get up.
ALIX	Where is Marcus?
ARBITER	Get up.
ALIX	I'm so cold.
ARBITER	Get up and I'll get you a blanket.
ALIX	I want to know where Marcus is.
ARBITER	Get up and I'll tell you where he is.
ALIX	I'm imagining this. You're haunting me.
ARBITER	Last time. Get up.

ALIX gets up.

ARBITER	How are your eyes?
ALIX	Fuck you. How's your pulse?
ARBITER	Alive and kicking.
ALIX	Shame.
ARBITER	Alix, I must inform you that your time in this facility has come to an end.
ALIX	The facility has come to an end.
ARBITER	If you could see, you'd know that's not the case. All in time.
ALIX	You're lying.
ARBITER	Your progress has been slow. Non-existent. And you have proved yourself completely unwilling to convert.

ALIX	I'm gay.
ARBITER	You're sick.
ALIX	So are you.
ARBITER	Beyond help.
ALIX	Thank fuck.
ARBITER	Subsequently, you will be going to the Other Place.
ALIX	No.
ARBITER	Yes.
ALIX	I can't.
ARBITER	You can. You will.
ALIX	I have to wait for Marcus.
ARBITER	Oh yes. Him.
ALIX	I promised him/
ARBITER	Yes.
ALIX	I have to wait/
ARBITER	This is unnecessary.
ALIX *(Beat)*	Unnecessary. What the fuck have you done with him? If you've hurt him/
ARBITER	Unnecessary because he doesn't exist.
ALIX	What?
ARBITER	Alix, when I said that your entire time in this facility will be a test of your resolve to return to the society I meant it. The Marcus you have held, kissed, sodomised, shared and apparently cared for does not exist. Very convincing I grant you but a well

formulated simulation.

ALIX   I... don't... believe you.

ARBITER   Yes, you do. I told you when you arrived here Alix that everything would be a test. We couldn't just rely on treatment. We needed to test your progress as we went along. With temptation. Could you make the right choice. Even as a hole is blown in the facility offering you escape – could you do the right thing?

The ARBITER produces a clicker and clicks through the sound effects heard in the play.

ARBITER   Clever, isn't it?

Suddenly, it plays "This is a test. This is a test."

ARBITER   That one was my idea. They said it was too on the nose but I wanted to give you one last chance before you fucked him.

ALIX *(through whimpers)* Love...

ARBITER   You can't say we didn't give you every chance. We gave you every chance. Marcus gave you every chance. You failed at every turn. The bomb simulation is particularly impressive, don't you think? Technology is a wonder. Imagine what the future may be like. What we'll be capable of. The mind boggles.

ALIX   I'm so cold.

ARBITER   Yes. You will be.

ALIX   I felt him though. I felt him against me. I felt myself inside him.

ARBITER   How else could we truly test you?

ALIX   A test.

ARBITER   Alix I know you won't believe this but I'm sorry. We're sorry.

ALIX   We?

ARBITER   Every single person from the society who you'll never see again. I grew fond of you I must say and I'm most sorry you couldn't be helped.

ALIX   I bet nobody makes it back, do they? You just torture people and then send them to the Other Place.

ARBITER   Like I say, it's been a pleasure.

ALIX   I'm freezing.

ARBITER   It's nearly time.

ALIX   I want/

ARBITER   Now is a time to be silent.

Silence.

After a time, ALIX opens his mouth wide.

ARBITER   For old time's sake.

ALIX   Are there lots of people there?

ARBITER   Where?

ALIX   In the Other Place.

ARBITER   Alix, it's about time you started to see more clearly, isn't it?

ALIX   What?

ARBITER   Say it.

ALIX   I can't.

ARBITER   Say it.

ALIX   Please.

ARBITER   You're afraid?

ALIX   Please.

ARBITER   There is no Other Place. It ends here.

ALIX   What ends?

ARBITER   All of it. All the sickness, all the pain. It
all ends here.

ALIX   Is it quick?

ARBITER   As quick as you'd like it to be.

ALIX   I can decide.

ARBITER   You can. A last enduring luxury. A
moment of bliss before oblivion.

ALIX   Why?

ARBITER   Karma.

ALIX laughs hysterically.

ARBITER   Are you ready?

ALIX   Take me now.

ARBITER   We're already here. Open your eyes.

*As ALIX opens his eyes, he is in a spotlight. He can
see again. The ARBITER is gone. A light fades up on a
dressing table stage left. It is small and antique, on it sits
a selection of lipstick, eye shadow, eye liner and mascara.
Hanging on the small mirror is a mop head. ALIX knows
instinctively what to do. He moves to the table, sits, and
begins to apply the make-up, thick like a clown. When he
is finished, he takes the mop head and fixes it to his head.
He looks in the mirror and smiles – it is not enough. He*

takes the lipstick and broadens the smile. He turns and looks over his shoulder as a light fades up on an old, dried out but filthy toilet, centre stage. Another light fades up on an up-turned mop handle in front of it. He gets up and moves towards it. He steps into the toilet and stares out.

The sound of an old record player turning begins and then Barbra Streisand singing "Happy Days Are Here Again (1963 version from THE BARBRA STREISAND ALBUM)" begins to play timidly. ALIX picks up the handle and bittersweetly, and cathartically, performs the song. It starts as a nostalgic grotesque lip sync, every inch of the movement Streisand performed, by a clown. Half way through ALIX abandons the toilet, and as the set dressings dissolve away, he makes his way down to take the stage himself, singing the remainder of the song as himself.

ALIX *(Sings)*

So long sad times
Go long bad times
We are rid of you at last
howdy gay times
cloudy gray times
You are now a thing of the past

Happy days are here again
the skies above are clearer again
so let's sing a song of cheer again
Happy days are here again

Altogether shout it now
There's no one
who can doubt it now

So let's tell the world about it now
Happy days are here again
Your cares and troubles are gone

There'll be no more from now on
from now on

Happy days are here again
the skies above are so clear again
so, let's sing a song of cheer again
Happy times
Happy nights
Happy days
are here again

As he finishes there is thunderous and deafening applause.

The same sound of the bomb from earlier plays to drown it out until there is nothing but a distant rumbling.

ALIX slowly rocks back and forth on stage taking large breaths which turn into gasps. His eyes are wide. He is terrified.

As he gasps the lights fade to black and the rumbling fades out, leaving only darkness and the echoing sound of ALIX, gasping for air. For some time, we continue to hear the gasping until, at last, it stops.

He goes to the Other Place.

Lights down.

The End.